CHILDHOOD OF KALAM

Greatness is not by accident.

Greatness is a quality processed, honed and learnt over a lifetime of learning and hard work. Great human beings are built when a curious mind is met with life changing lessons, often early in the childhood. Just like the nature and quality of a tree is decided by the characteristic of the seed and how it is sown, the worth of a human life is shaped in the early stage of childhood.

We all know Dr. Kalam as an eminent teacher, an excellent President, an exception scientist, a talented rocket scientist, a team man, an institution builder and a man of ethics and integrity. But what went behind the scenes, in the formative days of 'Little Kalam' which shaped him slowly but surely into Dr. Kalam – the man we remember and admire.

This books aspires to take you in this early history of childhood of Kalam tracking 'Little Kalam' as he begins his first steps into the sands of Rameshwaram – which one day will translate into a march to the Rashtrapati Bhawan.

Srijan Pal Singh is a gold medallist MBA holder from IIM Ahmedabad and a social entrepreneur involved in evolving sustainable development systems.

He was Former Advisor and OSD to the Dr. A.P.J. Abdul Kalam, 11th President of India.

He has written over 12 books. Out of which he has co-authored 3 books with Dr. Kalam.

Currently he is CEO and Founding Member of Dr. A.P.J. Abdul Kalam Centre.

CHILDHOOD OF KALAM

(Stories based on Dr. A.P.J. Abdul Kalam's Childhood)

Srijan Pal Singh

PRABHAT PRAKASHAN

Published by
PRABHAT PRAKASHAN PVT. LTD.
4/19 Asaf Ali Road,
New Delhi-110 002 (INDIA)
e-mail: prabhatbooks@gmail.com

ISBN 978-93-86231-95-6
CHILDHOOD OF KALAM
by Srijan Pal Singh

Edition
2025

Price
₹ 250.00 (Rupees Two Hundred Fifty only)

Printed at
Narula Printers, Delhi

Dedicated to values and culture of Indian civilization, which throughout its ages, has taught every child of India the power of truth, integrity and undying hope.

Author's Note

Greatness is not by accident.

Greatness is a quality processed, honed and learnt over a lifetime of learning and hard work. Great human beings are built when a curious mind is met with life changing lessons, often early in the childhood. Just like the nature and quality of a tree is decided by the characteristic of the seed and how it is sown, the worth of a human life is shaped in the early stage of childhood.

Often these life teachings as a growing up child, transform into the values which set the boundaries of one's adult actions and govern one's decisions.

We all know Dr. Kalam as an eminent teacher, an excellent President, an exception scientist, a talented rocket scientist, a team man, an institution builder and a man of ethics and integrity. But what went behind the scenes, in the formative days of "Little Kalam" which shaped him slowly but surely into Dr. Kalam – the man we remember and admire.

This books aspires to take you in this early history of childhood of Kalam tracking "Little Kalam" as he begins his first steps into the sands of Rameshwaram – which one day will translate into a march to the Rashtrapati Bhawan.

Courage to Give

Courage to think different,
Courage to invent,
Courage to discover the impossible,
Courage to travel into an unexplored path,
Courage to share knowledge,
Courage to remove pain,
Courage to reach the unreached,
Courage to combat problems,
And succeed,
Are the unique qualities of youth.
As the youth of my nation,
I will work and work with courage to achieve success in all my missions.

—Dr. A.P.J. Abdul Kalam

Contents

Birth of Little Kalam

Today, Jainulabdeen and Ashiamma were happy to be blessed with a child. It was October 15,1931. The mother was lying inside the room with the newborn, while Jainulabdeen was out in the courtyard. He looked up to thank the Heavens for their baby boy. As his eyes grazed the skies, he spotted the imposing tower of the Ramanathaswamy Temple. The dazzling metal tower reflected the sun as if showering him with blessings.

"May he grow to be as glorious as these sunrays!" Jainulabdeen murmured.

Just then, the air reverberated with Azan—the call for the afternoon prayers —from the mosque. Not long after, the temple bells started ringing. All these holy signs around made the occasion divine.

□

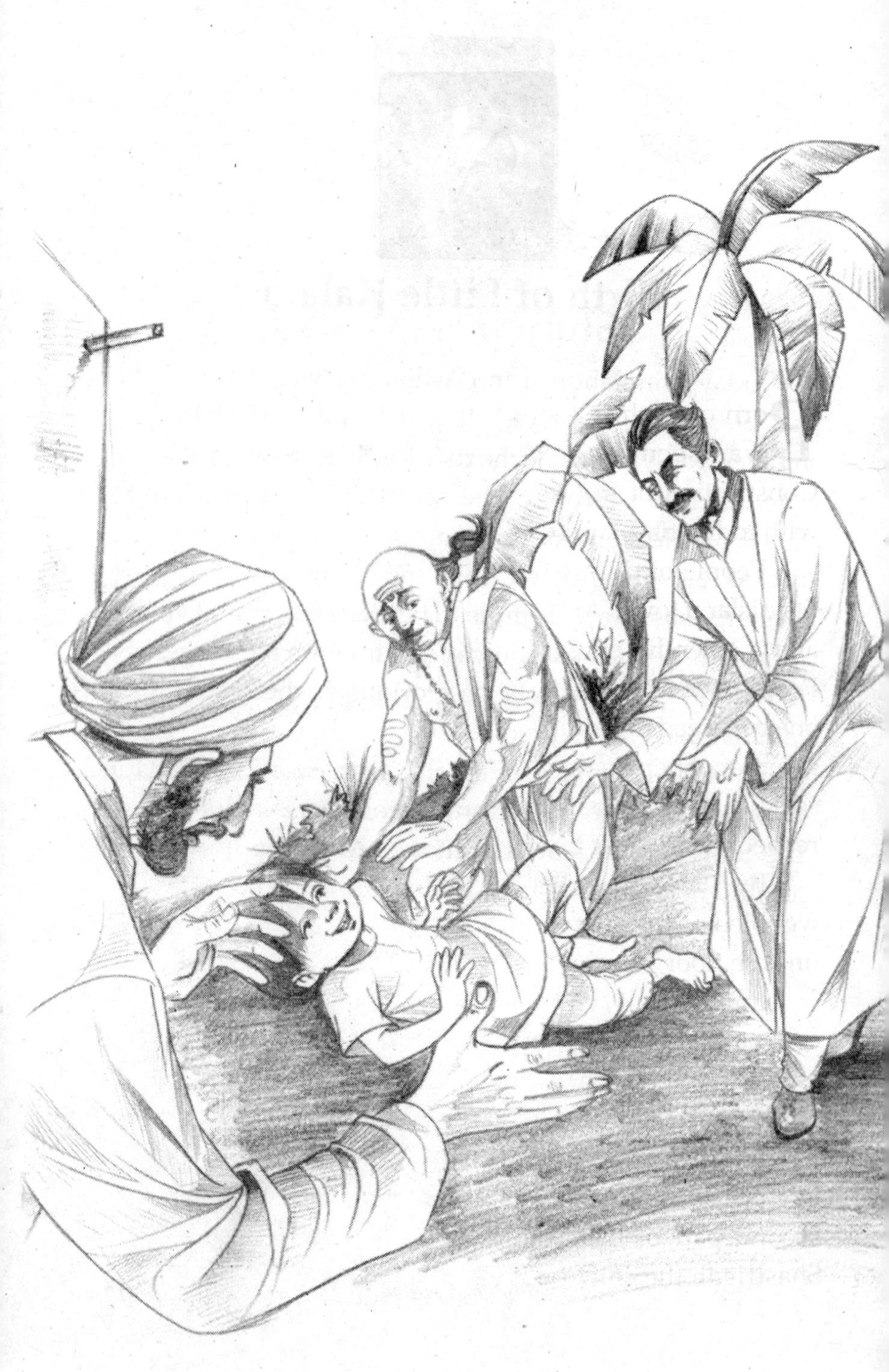

Stumbling Feet

Born on 15th October 1931, Little Kalam's birthplace was secular in its essence as reflected in the Constitution of India, though it was yet to be realized, with India still 16 years from being an independent nation.

People of different religions and faiths lived in this little island town. An imposing temple, a majestic mosque and a splendid church graced this town with blessings. People here lived in harmony. It didn't matter whether one belonged to Hinduism, Islamor Christianity. That was a matter of personal practice. Instead, when they mingled socially, they did as members of society, responsible and respectful towards one another.

By 1934, little Kalam was three years old. As he wobbled on the dusty courtyard, balancing himself on the uneven floor, he stumbled on the doorway and fell down.

Immediately, all eyes were on the child. He did not cry, neither did he make any attempt to stand up. He looked around for help and found not one but three pairs of hands...reaching out to help him.

Little Kalam's eyes brightened up and his teeth shone like pearls. The first pair of hands was his father's. The second pair of hands was that of Pakshi Lakshamana Shastrigal, the chief priest of Rameswaram Temple and the last pair of hands was that of Rev. Father Bodal, the priest of St. Antony's Church.

The three were friends and often met at the square not far from Little Kalam's house to discuss matters pertaining to the town.

It was Rev. Father Bodal who picked up Little Kalam. "O my son! Did you hurt yourself?"

By then, Little Kalam had forgotten all about the fall. Instead, he pointed at the pilgrims walking down the street in their bright saffron costumes.

"They are going in search of God," said Fr. Bodal.

Little Kalam smiled a full smile as if he understood everything.

This was the atmosphere in which Little Kalam grew up—under affectionate and watchful eyes.

□

Little Kalam Goes to School

Little Kalam was now a whole of six years. He went to an Arabic School every morning. Since his father wanted to inculcate in him secular qualities, he also went to the Panchayat Elementary School.

As Little Kalam started learning, he was always the first to raise his hand to any question in class. He had a curious mind too, often asking questions unexpected of a child of his age. While he learnt several subjects and languages, he found science to be the most interesting. In fact, all the students in his class loved science. This can be attributed to the teachers who explained things simply, drawing relevant examples from their immediate surroundings. This helped students to absorb the laws and theories of science easily.

□

The Lanka Bridge

As the three religious men sat at the town square talking, their eyes followed a child picking up stones from all over and arranging them in a neat row. He was Little Kalam.

"What are you doing?" Fr. Bodal asked. Little Kalam did not respond. When Fr. Bodal asked a second time, he said promptly, "Building a bridge!"

"What bridge?" the Father asked affectionately.

Little Kalam looked for words to articulate what he had in mind but ended up mumbling something. Finally, he put one hand behind his back like a tail and the other in the air before dancing around in circles.

"What is he doing?" Fr. Bodal wondered.

"Let me see," said Shastrigal. He walked up to the child and bent down to ask him, "Hanumana?"

The child nodded his head excitedly and continued to dance. Just two days ago, Shastrigal had told him the story of how Hanumana had built the bridge to Lanka with the help of his monkey brigade.

When Shastrigal told Janab Jainulabdeen about the bridge, the three laughed their hearts out.

□

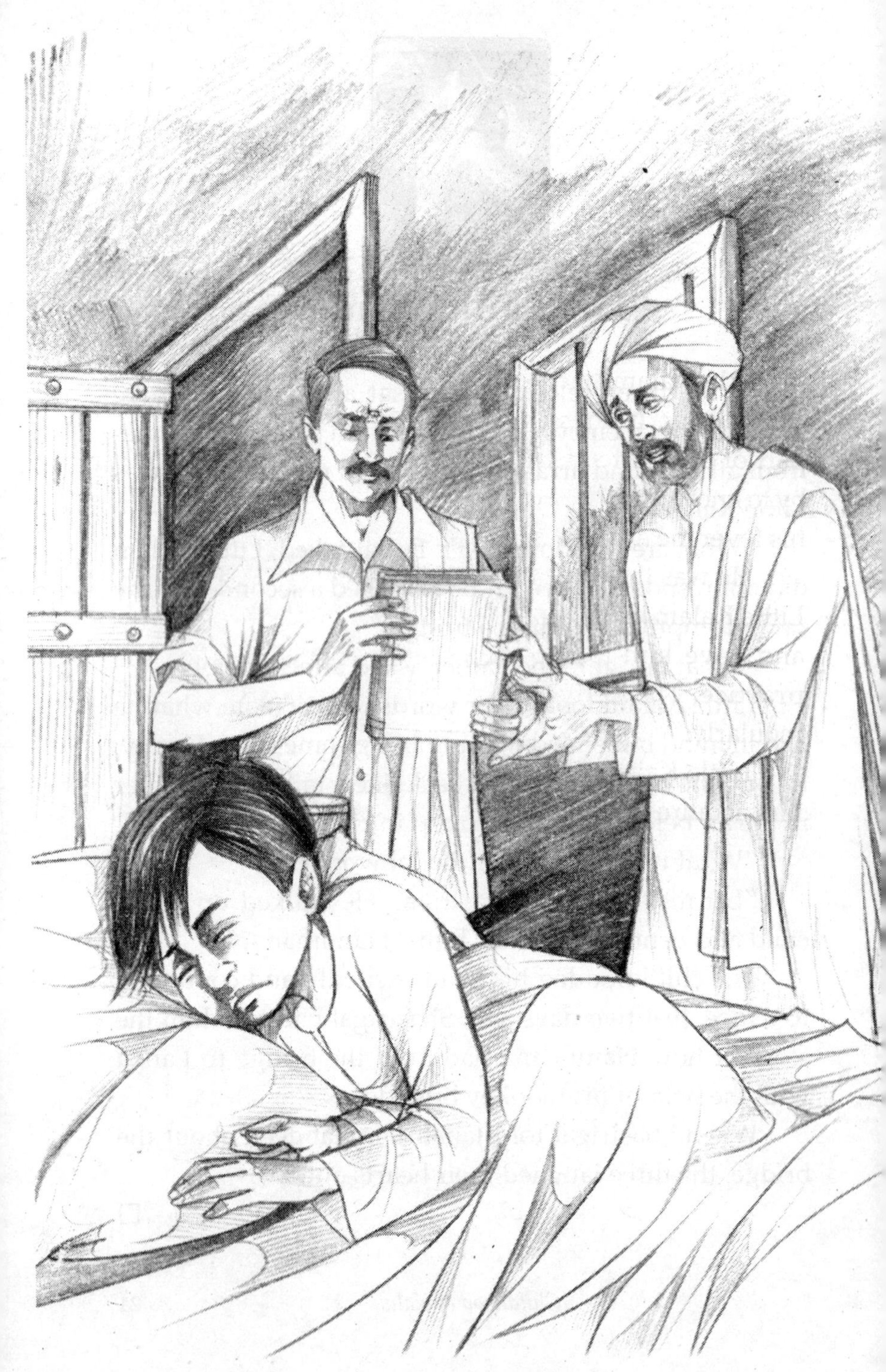

Caring Teacher

Little Kalam had fever and could not go to school oneday. In those days, teachers treated students as part of their extended families. So, Muthu Iyer dropped by to know what the matter was. When he found out about his fever, he advised on the treatment.

He was the same teacher who, when he noticed that Little Kalam had poor handwriting, went up to his father and gave him a three-page work sheet for longhand practice. He said, "Make sure he does the exercise regularly."

Little Kalam was grateful to this teacher for helping him acquire good habits early on in life.

□

Building the Boat

A huge number of Hindu pilgrims visiting the town of Rameswaram needed to be ferried across the sea. It was a thriving business. So Jainulabdeen decided to build a ferry boat to ferry pilgrims to Dhanushkodi. He started building the boat at the seashore and a relative, Ahmed Jallaluddin, assisted him.

Little Kalam kept going to the seashore to check the progress. He watched how the two men worked on the boat and how—with every passing day—it assumed the required shape. The first step was to build the underlying framework, on which the planks were to be laid from one end to another.

One day, when Little Kalam went to the seashore, he was shocked to see that Jallaluddin was trying to burn down the boat. His father was working on some planks and was looking the other way.

"Stop, stop that..." he cried out to draw his father's attention.

Both his father and Jallaluddin looked at him in surprise.

"What's wrong?" Jallaluddin asked in his usual polite manner.

"What are you doing? You are burning down the boat, aren't you?" asked Little Kalam, perplexed to see that his father was not reacting.

"O that... I am not burning it, I am seasoning it," said Jallaluddin assuringly.

He then called the child and showed him how seasoning made the wood sturdier. He explained why it was necessary to make the wood strong so that it could withstand the saline water in the sea.

Jallaluddin showed him the difference between soft wood, hard wood and flexible wood. It was indeed a lesson for Little Kalam.

Perhaps it was this lesson that helped him classify metals to be used as different parts of the huge satellites and missiles that he was destined to build in the future.

□

Ferry Lessons

Little Kalam had very little free time. Since he had to wake up early, he needed to go to bed early. He attended the Arabic School before going to the regular school. After this, he would often enjoy reading his books. Though he was still a child,. he was little interested in playing with children of his age. But, Sundays and holidays were different. He had a lot of time in hand.

The ferry boat was ready by now and Janab Jainulabdeen employed some oarsmen to sail it. This business earned him good money. The pilgrims came in hordes and throughout the year.

It was on holidays that Little Kalam would look for an opportunity to hop into the ferry. He would often hide himself in the crowd until the boat left the shore. He was afraid that Jallaluddin or his father would refuse to let him go.

Little Kalam loved the sea. The rising waves and the flying seagulls fascinated him. But what particularly fascinated him were the conversations of the pilgrims who came from across India. Sometimes there would be foreigners too. They spoke different languages, and often spoke Hindi and English in a range of accents.

Little Kalam enjoyed those conversations. This was how he learnt about several things happening in the country and the world. He came to know not only about Hindu mythology—how Lord Rama rescued Sita and how the good prevailed over the evil—but also current events. He came to know of the ongoing freedom movement in the country and often wondered why the British dealt with the Indians heartlessly.

It was during one of these trips that he came to know about Japan's attack on China and how that could lead to a world war again.

These experiences had a lifelong influence on Little Kalam. Apart from the conversations, there were occasions when everybody would be quiet on the boat. Such silence was often common when the waves were high and furious. Little Kalam was seldom afraid of the lashing waves. He would look at the sea and try to figure out the rhythm.

□

Little Kalam Learns about Flight

Little Kalam had a passion for birds. What fascinated him was the majestic way in which birds soared and glided in the air above the open sea. He often wondered how birds could flap their wings and rise into the air. He was even more interested to find out how birds could glide in the air with their wings spread out and still.

It was 1941. He was 10 years old now. That day, the topic of discussion in class was birds. As the teacher explained the anatomy of a bird, Little Kalam asked, "How do birds fly?"

His science teacher, Siva Subramania looked at him in appreciation. A bird's diagram was already on the blackboard. He deviated from the topic and said, "Okay, let us first find out how birds fly."

He then carefully explained how a bird's wings, tail, body and head played a role in flying, how birds glide, and why they fly in a flock.

While the teacher tried his best to explain the concept of avian flight, the children, including Little Kalam, found it hard to grasp.

Meanwhile, the bell rang and the class got over. The teacher asked, "Do you now understand how birds fly?"

The students looked at each other. One hand rose up. "Yes, Abdul, stand up," said the teacher.

"I haven't understood a word," said Little Kalam.

"Okay, I'll explain it again tomorrow," said the teacher before leaving.

The next day, Siva Subramania once again explained all about the avian flight. When he realized the young students were still struggling, he suggested, "Let us go to the seashore!"

There the teacher showed the flying birds, going up and down, and explained how they were able to do so. Abdul closely observed the birds, their flapping wings and twisting tails along with the movement of their beaks. He was able to grasp the concept better, but he still had one question. "Why do birds fold their legs backwards?"

"To allow themselves to sail through the air unhindered," said the teacher with a smile.

While everybody in class now understood the concept better, it would stay with Little Kalam for all times to come. When he walked back to school, the other children got busy playing, but Little Kalam had something else in mind. Maybe he was thinking beyond avian flight.

□

Breaking Barriers

Little Kalam was a Muslim boy, while most of his teachers were orthodox Brahmins. The caste system among the Hindus is quite rigid. So there is little chance of people from different castes eating together, let alone eating with people of other faiths. Nonetheless, there were people who wanted to get rid of the caste system, and many of them were from amongst the Brahmins. One such person was Little Kalam's teacher, Siva Subramania Iyer.

Siva Subramania had a very conservative wife, who would not allow any 'unwanted' person in her house, especially in her kitchen. She had a traditional household where people ate in the kitchen. It simply meant that people from other castes and religions could not eat in the house. But, here was this teacher who wanted to eradicate this age-old system.

In his bid to break social barriers with the zeal of a rebel, Siva Subramania invited Little Kalam, his most promising student, to eat at his house. In Little Kalam, he saw the promise of someone who could compete with children in the big cities and who could outshine all others in his field.

Siva Subramania got Little Kalam seated in the courtyard and approached his wife. "I have a little guest

with me. I have invited him to a meal," he told his wife in a slow, careful but confident voice.

As the wife looked at the little boy with a skull cap, she was furious, but somehow she controlled herself and said, "No way..." She was totally taken aback at the very idea of serving food to a Muslim boy in her kitchen.

"He is my guest," said Siva Subramania unruffled.

"Okay, if you say so, but I won't let him into my kitchen; it has to be outside the kitchen," she said.

"That's not a bad idea," said Siva Subramania, as he spread the sheet on the floor just outside the kitchen. He served Little Kalam himself and sat down beside him. They ate together, while the wife looked in disbelief from behind the kitchen door.

They had boiled rice and *sambar* served on a leaf-plate. Little Kalam found it as tasty as the food cooked by his own mother. As he ate, drank water, cleaned the floor and washed his hands, he glanced at the two prying eyes behind the kitchen door and wondered if he and Siva Subramania ate differently, drank water differently, or cleaned the floor differently.

As Little Kalam stood up to leave after a happy meal, though under the watchful and perturbing gaze of his mentor's wife from behind the kitchen door, he said, "May I leave now?"

"Did you enjoy the food?" asked Siva Subramania.

Little Kalam mumbled, in fact, he could not decide whether to praise the food or say something about his wife.

"You might not have found the food tasty, especially because of the way you were treated," said Siva

Subramania in a didactic style, adding, "Yet you have to bear with such situations if you want to break barriers."

Little Kalam nodded. He was about to turn away, when Siva Subramania said, "You must learn to overcome the difficulty, and not get overcome by it. You can hope for a victory only when you decide to confront a situation."

"Yes, Sir," said Little Kalam.

"You will again come for a meal next week," said Siva Subramania.

Little Kalam smiled softly. He already admired his teacher, but now he found him worth glorifying.

□

Little Kalam Dines Again

When Siva Subramania invited him to his house for a second meal, he was not sure if it would actually happen. After school, as he packed up to go home, Siva Subramania approached him and said, "You are coming with me. We'll eat together today."

Little Kalam nodded his head softly. He did not know what to say. As they walked together, his favourite teacher kept talking to him all the way. He wanted to share as much knowledge and virtue as he could with this child who displayed such extraordinary promise. Meanwhile, Little Kalam wondered if his teacher's wife would allow him to have a second meal at their house.

Little Kalam had some surprise in store for him this time. The wife not only welcomed him into the house, but also took him inside the kitchen. The teacher and the pupil sat together, while the wife served them herself; this time, her eyes glowed with natural warmth and affection. Little Kalam did not find any difference between his teacher's wife and his mother. He could see the barriers breaking down.

It was a great lesson for Little Kalam and would stay with him throughout his life. Harmony can be cultivated only through bold little steps.

□

The Tempest

It was October 1942 and India was rising to demand self-rule under the overall leadership of Gandhiji. The Quit India Movement was in the offing. It could mean a great upheaval in the country. With the Second World War already on, America's entry in the scene had been further devastating. As far as life in this remote island was concerned, something else was about to be more devastating. It was a cyclone that hit the Bay of Bengal.

Little Kalam was doing his homework in the courtyard, when he felt the swiftness in the wind. He found it hard to control the flying pages. He kept books and stones on the flapping pages of his notebook to hold the pages down. Gradually, he realized that he could not do it. Little Kalam was a brilliant boy, and this was the reason that his teacher often assigned him extra homework. At this point, he was doing his extra homework.

When he found it hard to keep the pages under control, he decided to move into a room. He picked up the books and notebooks and walked into the room. When he returned to take his bag, he found it flying away in the violent wind. He ran after it, but the wind seemed to push him away. He reached his bag with a little difficulty and hurried back into the room. As he looked at the sky, he could see things flying everywhere—paper, clothes, objects, tin shades—under the dark, monstrous clouds. The wind got stronger. A cyclone was all set to hit the town.

Soon, it started pouring. The wind seemed determined to raze everything to the ground. As Ashiamma asked Little Kalam to sit tight inside the room, he thought about all those who were in the open sea. It was a little fishing town, and at any given time, there were several fishermen in the sea catching fish for their livelihood. He also thought of his father's boat and was thankful his father was not in the boat.

The lashing wind and waves devastated the town. Trees, houses and fields were laid waste by the furious winds and lashing waves. Jainulabdeen's boat was one of the victims of the cyclone. His coconut grove was razed to the ground. Both sources of income for the family were destroyed.

Little Kalam was sad at the destruction. He remembered how quickly his father climbed up the coconut trees to pluck coconuts. 'How will he do it now?' he asked himself.

Little Kalam could no longer steal his way into the ferry boat. As the family gathered in the courtyard, looking tense and worried, Jainulabdeen said in a calm and assuring way, "You receive the fruit of your doing."

Then he started explaining what misfortune meant in his faith. It is no great thing for man to be confronted with a calamity. This is the way God tests people. God teaches us to resign ourselves to our misfortune. We cannot receive anything, nor can we lose anything without His desire; everything moves as per His decree. When man faces calamity, he should be patient. And when he receives something, he should be thankful, for without his grace, man can receive nothing. He is omniscient and omnipotent. No leaf can move without his wish.

□

Rebuilding the Boat

Little Kalam had seen how the boat had been built. Memories of it were still fresh in his mind. He recalled how the wood was seasoned and shaped just a few years back. He was a little grown up now, and if his father decided to build another boat, he could perhaps help him to some extent, he thought.

Jainulabdeen always taught his children to be self-reliant. When you help yourself, the Divine one opens your path to resources from which you can benefit, he said to Little Kalam one day.

Jainulabdeen salvaged all that he could from the old, damaged boat, and set himself to the task of building a new one. Building it was no easy task. It was at that time when the British ruled over India and provided no relief to the cyclone victims or victims of other natural calamities. Seeing his poor financial state, no one was willing to give a loan to his father to rebuild the boat. So, he decided to build the boat by himself from whatever little was available within his resources.

As Little Kalam saw the boat take shape gradually, he had more questions to ask about the quality of wood, the shape of the boat and what made it stay afloat on the water. His inquisitive mind was always looking for answers. He always got Jallaluddin to answer to his queries. Whenever Jallaluddin did not know an answer, he never tried to evade it. He would briefly say, "I will come back to you." On most occasions, he tried to find answers from the newspapers and books at his disposal. On few occasions, he had no resource to find answers, and he admitted his inability. You will appreciate that Jallaluddin had studied only up to the eighth standard, yet he had wide knowledge of things.

Little Kalam, however, had other sources – his teachers. Whatever he understood from their explanations, he would discuss them with Jallaluddin. This was how he had started to build a closer affinity and bond with him.

One day, Little Kalam asked Jallaluddin, "Why should you use teak to build the boat?"

"It is strong and dense wood. Moreover, white ants don't pose a threat to it," said Jallaluddin.

"Why do white ants not pose a threat to it?" Little Kalam promptly came up with another question.

Jallaluddin thought for a while and said, "No idea. I don't know."

Whenever Jallaluddin could not answer a question, Little Kalam made a mental note of it. Next day, as the recess bell rang and his science teacher was about to walk out of the class, Little Kalam asked, "Sir, why do white ants not eat teak?"

The teacher tapped his shoulder and while he walked outside the class, he said, "If you taste teak, you will know the answer."

"But you don't eat wood, do you?"

The teacher smiled and said, "Of course, you don't eat wood, but you can certainly taste it. As far as teak is concerned, it is bitter. So, white ants do not like the taste."

"Thank you, Sir," said Little Kalam.

"And it has a lesson for you," said the teacher.

Little Kalam looked up with an enquiring eye. "You have a lesson to learn from teak's bitter taste. If you have enemies, you ought to inculcate such qualities in you that your enemies would not be able to harm you."

"Yes, Sir," said Little Kalam. In his delicate mind, he was planning how to explain this moral lesson to Jallaluddin along with the mystery of why white ants don't eat teak.

□

Little Kalam Eats His Mother's Share

It was the time of Second World War in early 1940s. Millions of lives were getting lost in the battlefield. In addition, many more people lost their lives as the aeroplanes from both sides bombed civilian areas senselessly.

Ironically, Britain led the Allied forces and fought with the Axis powers in the name of liberty and freedom; but it was the same country that had enslaved a large number of countries in Asia and Africa, bringing untold miseries on them.

Of course, India had to face the brunt of its imperialistic bias, as it had been forced into the Second World War. Britain recruited a lot of Indian young men to deploy them in different war zones in India and abroad. Not only this, they exploited all types of resources for the war, including natural, industrial and agricultural resources. India was already beginning to face the pressures of the global war. Food was rationed; a large number of people did not get to eat a full meal, and nutrition was far below the expected standards.

Little Kalam was not free from the impact of this situation. As the supply of food grains was rationed, people had to make do with what they got. In his family, the food was consciously limited so that they could manage till the next time. The situation was pitiable. It was hard for the elders to explain to the young why they could not be given enough food. Often, parents, especially mothers, sacrificed their share for the sake of their children.

Usually, Little Kalam did not enjoy playing. He loved reading while children of his age at home and outside loved playing and being noisy. That day, he did not have anything to read, so he too decided to play. He enjoyed himself and was tired and hungry by dinner time.

That month, rice was in short supply, which was the family's staple food. So, they had to make do with *chapattis* made from wheat. They did not relish them, but they had little choice.

Little Kalam was hungry and he sat near the fireplace where his mother was making the *chapattis*. All the family members sat in a small circle; each of them was expected to eat three; it was an unwritten rule, and everybody followed it without a word; violating it meant one of them was sure to go hungry. Little Kalam was oblivious of this rule. When he had eaten all three of his share, his mother asked, "Do you need more?" Little Kalam nodded.

"Have this," said Ashiamma with an affectionate smile on her face.

Little Kalam did not understand why his elder brother looked at him sternly. He finished eating the *chapatti* and his mother asked again, "One more?"

"Yes, Mother," said Little Kalam.

Little Kalam ate a total of six *chapattis*, he could have eaten more, he thought.

As Little Kalam got up and walked to his bed, his elder brother said, "You are stupid." It is because of you that Mother has to go hungry tonight."

"Why?"

"Everybody was supposed to eat three *chapattis*, but you ate six, you kept eating and Mother kept giving you her share, what a blockhead you are!"

Now only Little Kalam realized what he had done. He turned and went to his mother, who had only a little *sambar* in a bowl. He cried and took her in his arms. "You have to sleep on a hungry stomach, all because of me," he wailed.

"No, my son, No," said Ashiamma, "When I see my children eating, my hunger is satisfied."

Little Kalam had lessons to learn from this episode: Mothers were the most sacrificing beings in the world; they had to be considerate even when people were acting against their interests.

☐

First Income

Little Kalam could perceive the financial constraints f the family owing to the combined causes of Second World War and cyclone. Jainulabdeen was not the one to be disheartened by such challenges. He soon started to work on a new boat.

Little Kalam realized he was now growing up and could help his father tide over the difficult times to some extent. He had no idea why tamarind seeds were in such demand. So, he went from door to door collecting tamarind seeds and selling them to the local grocery store. He earned an amount of one *anna*, a princely sum in those days. One *anna* is equal to six paise, or one-sixteenth of a rupee. In those days, one *anna* could feed a man for a day.

But, this business could not go on indefinitely. There were not many opportunities to gather tamarind seeds from households, but it taught him a lesson that anything could be helpful to tide over difficult times.

□

First Real Income

When God puts you through difficult times, he also shows you a way out. For some strange reason, the British government suspended the train stop at the Rameswaram railway station, even though it faced no threats during the Second World War.

Since the trains allowed a lot of people to earn their livelihood, it had a huge impact on many households. Samsuddin, Little Kalam's cousin, was one of them. He was a newspaper vendor, who brought newspapers from Pamban, off loaded it at Rameswaram and distributed them to his customers. The suspension of the train halt threatened his business. He had a creative idea to handle the situation. He called Little Kalam and sought his help, "Abdul, you have a chance to earn money."

This possibility brightened up Little Kalam's eyes. His business in tamarind seeds was not at all attractive.

"Look, now the train doesn't halt at our local station," said Samsuddin.

"Yes, I know," said Little Kalam.

"It means I cannot bring newspapers to the town," Samsuddin said.

"You can throw it from the running train," said Little Abdul.

"That's what I have thought about," said Samsuddin, but then it has its problems, explained Samsuddin. "If I throw the papers and then come back from Dhanushkodi to collect them, it would be late afternoon. Nobody would then want to buy or read a newspaper. No one wants stale news."

"What can I do? How can I help you?"

"It is simple, you have to pick up the newspapers and distribute them to the readers," said Samsuddin.

Little Kalam found the offer attractive. He earned some money in the fray, but it did to him another good. He had close proximity to newspapers. He often opened a spare newspaper and looked at its different pages. He had not yet mastered the language, but the pictures described many things. His comprehension of the world around had started to grow. This also made him ask Jallaluddin and his teachers more questions, which now covered almost all topics under the sun.

□

Delivering Newspapers

His first job of collecting and delivering newspapers was a challenging one. As soon as he returned from his Arabic School, he sprinted towards the railway station, keeping his eyes and ears open for any signs of the approaching train – Madras-Dhanushkodi Mail, which was seldom late. He often spotted its smoke rising in the horizon when he was still two-three hundred yards away, and he would run towards the platform trying to locate Samsuddin waving at him from the speeding train. As he got habituated, he found it rather easy.

Little Kalam admired the way Samsuddin threw the papers from the train. As soon as the train huffed and puffed away, Little Kalam's work started. He picked up the bundles, divided them into batches according to the neighbourhoods and off he went. The next one hour, he was running from one house to another. Often he found people waiting for him and many of them praised him for his effort. Seeing a cheerful eight-year-old boy running through his routine was a great sight.

After this, he returned home at about 8 a.m., when his mother would serve him breakfast. It was like nectar after the morning's hard work, but it was not yet over. He would then head for school.

The newspaper duty was on in the evening too, when he had to collect dues from the customers. Most of them paid him on the first call, but there were a few who would keep stalling the payment.

□

Father's Divine Connection

Jainulabdeen, Little Kalam's father, had a ferry boat for the pilgrims. His house was on the mosque street, not far away from the Shiva temple. As the town of Rameswaram was located on the east coast, the day dawned early, and with the early rays of the sun, the town came to life. His father was up early in the morning, when the humdrum of daily life was yet to start and the sound of the sea could be heard clearly.

Little Kalam too was up early to attend the Arabic class. By the time he was up, his father would be getting ready to leave. Little Kalam knew his father's route. He would walk out of the house and, passing through narrow lanes, would come out on the broader road along the Shiva temple. Then, he would head for the open spaces to go to his coconut grove, which was about 4 km from the house.

A walk in the morning is part of a farmer's life. It is a good physical exercise too. But Little Kalam felt that the morning walks made his father's face shine in a strange glory...perhaps it was owing to his regular offering of prayers...he never missed his *namaz*.

On holidays, Little Kalam often accompanied his father to the mosque for prayers. "You must never miss

your prayers. It inculcates in you the motivation to not miss your duty," his father told him once.

Whenever his father came out of the mosque after prayers, he was surrounded by people outside. They were from different faiths. Jainulabdeen offered them solace with his words. He was neither a preacher nor a teacher. But, his conviction in God made people believe that he had some supernatural powers.

Many of these people held a bowl of water in which Jainulabdeen dipped his fingers reciting the name of God.

Once Little Kalam asked his father, "Can this water cure anything? Does it have magical powers?"

Jainulabdeen smiled and said, "This water is only venerated with the name of God. It has no power if it is not used with conviction. If people claim it can cure them, it is owing to their conviction in the name of God."

"Why do these people come to you? And what do you really do for them?"

"Whenever a person finds himself alone, he starts looking for a saviour, a companion. He needs him when he is in trouble. He looks for a special helper. I have no divine powers, but I pray for those who come to me. It makes me feel as if I am a go – between in their effort to find the Divine company," said Jainulabdeen.

"What is the best way to tackle problems?" the curious little boy asked.

"When you are faced with adversity, look within yourself, for He resides within you," said Jainulabdeen. "It gives you an opportunity for introspection, and this works for you."

Little Kalam had much to learn from this humble boat-owner. He assimilated this lesson early on in life and followed it all his life whenever he faced a problem. Introspection is the answer to several questions.

□

Morning Walks

"My teacher says that morning walks are good for health," said Little Kalam to his father.

"Yes, of course it is, but it is more than just that," said Jainulabdeen.

"How is it?"

"Nature is at its best in the morning. The chirping birds, the cool breeze, the golden red sky…all these are scenes that one mustn't miss. Everyday, you find Nature unfold herself, but everyday it is a different experience. With change in season, Nature brings to glory its different shades…it is marvellous in all its shades," said Jainulabdeen.

Little Kalam had a nice lesson to learn. This lesson stayed with him all his life. In course of his life, he had the opportunity to be at a large number of places…there were occasions when he had to sleep late, but never did he miss his morning walks…he felt that they instilled in him a sense of beauty and rejuvenated him.

□

How Little Kalam Ate

Little Kalam loved his mother dearly. She did especially dote on him, but his love for her came from her commitment to the household work. She would work as hard as she could.

Little Kalam had vivid memories of how he ate in the company of his family. He sat closest to his mother. She ensured that he ate well to face the vagaries of daily life which he had to go through right since early morning until the evening.

Abdul recalls how the family members sat on the kitchen floor together and ate off banana leaves. Usually, the menu included boiled rice, a bowl of delicious *sambar*, home-made pickles and coconut *chutney*. Rice was the staple food, while during the rationing period, rice was in short supply and *chapatti* replaced rice.

They ate after washing their hands, mouth and feet. They ate with their fingers, mixing the food well. Talking was not allowed while eating, but there was a lot of hullabaloo until everybody started eating. It was a time when children were free to interact with each other. Little Kalam had a sweet and mild way of talking. So his voice was often lost in the din, but his mother and Zohra made sure he was heard.

□

The Burnt *Chapatti*

Little Kalam's mother Ashiamma was tired that day. She had to wake up early as Jainulabdeen needed to leave early. She worked all day and by dinner time, she was thoroughly fatigued. Yet she could not rest, she had to cook dinner for the family. There was no rice that day, so she had to make *chapattis*, which meant more work. Nonetheless, she made the *chapattis* without any complain, while the family members sat in a semi-circle near the hearth.

She served the first piece of *chapatti* to Jainulabdeen, and it was a burnt one. Little Kalam noticed it. He was sure that his father would either admonish his wife or throw away the *chapatti*, but there was surprise in store for him. His father ate the *chapatti* happily. As he was about to eat the last bit of the *chapatti*, Ashiamma noticed it and immediately apologized. But, his father said, "I like burnt *rotis*."

This surprised Little Kalam. Later at night, when he went to his father to say good night, he could not help but ask, "Do you really love burnt *rotis*?"

Holding him in a warm hug, Jainulabdeen said, "Burnt *rotis* don't hurt, but harsh words do. You know, son, life is full of imperfect things...and imperfect people…I am not the best and am hardly good at anything! I forget birthdays and anniversaries just like anyone else. What I've learnt over the years is to accept each other's faults and choose to celebrate relationships."

Little Kalam learnt an important lesson that day. It is easy to criticize, but hard to provide solace.

□

Mother's Sacrifice

Little Kalam had to wake up early every morning to go to the Arabic School. He got up at quarter to five or so. The good thing about him was that his mother had to call him only once or twice. As he displayed an early aptitude for mathematics, his father arranged for tuitions from his mathematics teacher, starting from 4 a.m. It was already a little too early, but it became even harder with the condition that the teacher set. The four students he had agreed to teach, needed to reach his home at dawn only after a bath.

Little Kalam started his day while it was still pitch dark outside. Naturally, his mother had to wake him up on time. She would help him take a bath and direct him to his teacher's home.

Little Kalam was uncomfortable in the beginning, but his interest in mathematics kept him motivated. He would return from his tuition at 5 a.m., when he would once again have to hurry to the Arabic School not far from the house.

This went on for a year. And it was also the time he had to help Samsuddin run his newspaper business. After his Arabic class, he would run to the railway station. He

was lucky that the train – Madras-Dhanushkodi Mail – seldom got late. If it came late, it got difficult for him to reach school on time. The train fortunately stuck to its daily schedule and so did Little Kalam.

□

Sound of the Sea

The sea had a personality of its own. The land made its presence felt only rarely, through landslides and earthquakes; but the sea was a different case altogether. You could hear him all the time. He was never at rest. Sometimes he was mild, with the delicate rise and fall of the waves. The musical sound of the breaking waves was fascinating. Sometimes he hissed, especially during the spring tides. But this hissing was harmless, rather it had several gifts for the people living nearby.

After the spring tide returned, you could find several things on the shore, like fishes, animals, shells and pearls. Sometimes, the sea was angry; when he was angry, the simple realization is that man, despite all the scientific and technological progress he had made, remains at the mercy of a larger force that can crush his ambitions and plans in the blink of any eye.

Little Kalam grew up in close proximity to the sea. He was so used to land breezes and sea breezes; cyclones and tempests seemed to be part of his life. If the sea provided livelihood to his family and the ones around, it was the same sea that destroyed everything on occasions when he was angry. It had a lesson for Little Kalam that you had to rebuild to survive and that could be done only when you were ready to face your troubles.

□

Plus Points of Newspaper Vending

Little Kalam had a hectic schedule, which included his early morning mathematics tuition, Arabic School, newspaper distribution, regular school and some work at home in addition to his homework and collecting dues from the customers.

Collecting newspapers in the morning was a challenge. He could not collect bundles of newspapers without a keen sight. In a few days, as he grew taller with so much running around, he could judge distances quite accurately. It was also a practical lesson in mathematics, as he had to engage in calculating the money he had to give and take from customers.

Sundays were lazy mornings, but still educational. As he leisurely walked with the newspapers distributing them from one locality to another, there were people who would ask him about his work and ask him what was written in the newspapers. At times, he overheard what people talked about the current events that transpired in the world at that critical time of Second World War and Freedom Movement. He came to know more about Gandhiji, Congress, Hitler, Periyar E.V. Ramaswamy and other people and things.

Little Kalam's life had started to take shape for the better. It had a lesson for him, that of punctuality. Being a working man meant to be responsible and to be up and ready to face the day. Everything else could wait, but not the train. He had to be there at the railway station without fail.

□

Saving the Idol

Rameswaram was a quiet, sleepy town, often buzzing with hordes of pilgrims and tourists who came to visit the Ramanathswamy Temple. Mythologically, the Shiv Linga here was carved by Sita herself, and was of great importance for the Indians, who visited the town from across the country.

It was a Sunday and Little Kalam returned home after having distributed the newspapers. He finished his breakfast and stepped out. He wanted to play for a while, but the children were not yet ready. He found Jainulabdeen sitting in the courtyard over a cup of tea. He had seen a ceremony that day at the Ramanathswamy Temple in which a procession of the idol was being taken out for a sacred bath in the tank on the temple premises. He brought this to the notice of his father.

"Yes, it is very sacred for the Hindus," said Jainulabdeen. "It is like a ceremonial bath for the *Vigraha* or idol. Your forefathers were also connected with this ceremony."

It roused Little Kalam's interest. He asked, "How?"

The story that his father related went like this.

It was at the time of his great-great-grandfather. He was present to see the ceremony, and as the Brahmins dipped the idols into a tank, the idol slipped into the water. It was a calamity! People stood rooted in horror! It was at this critical hour that the great-great-grandfather of Little Kalam displayed his presence of mind. Without a second thought, he jumped into the tank, while people shrieked and screamed all around. Unperturbed, the forefather retrieved the idol, with the helping hands of the Brahmins. A great communal harmony was displayed. No one rued that the idol had been touched by a Muslim, rather everybody appreciated the hero, his forefather was treated like a hero.

In its proclamation, the temple decided that the hero would be given *Mudal Marayadai*, a rare honour given to only great servants of the temple. It meant that the temple would bestow its first honour on him on each festival day. This tradition continued for years. After him, his son continued to be honoured too.

□

A Calamity

Little Kalam went to school in his traditional dress, wearing a skull cap. So did all his friends as there was no prescribed school uniform. His closest friends were all Brahmins. He shared his desk with Ramanadhan, the son of Pakshi Lakshamana Shastrigal, the priest of the Ramanathswamy Temple. It was fun for the children to be together in and out of school.

As the two friends walked to school, Little Kalam noticed that the school's brick and mortar building had a thatched roof. It was not a sturdy structure, and with the sea close by, it could be razed to ground in a cyclone. But, calamity was nowhere in their horizon. They were there to enjoy themselves and had no idea what was in store for them.

The school did not have quite so many facilities, but it was certainly the place where the teachers taught with dedication. They paid personal attention to every student. To pay equal attention to over 50 students in class was not an easy task. They taught not only to help their students to score well, but also tried their best to help them develop love for the subjects. If a student was absent one day, one or the other teacher was sure to visit his house to find out what was wrong. A bright student was praised

by the teacher. Also, the teacher would spread the word about the brightest students when in town.

Little Kalam had a lesson to learn from this: great education does not come from great facilities or a huge building, or great advertisements. It comes from the way education is imparted; teachers make all the difference.

But, that day was a tough lesson for Little Kalam.

Perfect harmony prevailed in the town of Rameswaram. People of all castes and religions lived in complete harmony. Little Kalam shared his seat with Ramanadhan, a Brahmin. Both of them attended school in their traditional attire.

Soon there was a talk that a new teacher was coming. In a small school, it was big news. There were questions abound: will he be strict? Will he be considerate? Will he answer their queries patiently?

When the teacher finally walked into the class in a Brahmin attire, everybody stood up.

"Sit down," said the new teacher affectionately. And then he quickly glanced across the class to gauge the caste of students by what they were wearing. Little Kalam, too, observed the grave look.

The teacher's eyes grazed from the back benchers—probably presuming they would be the naughtiest—to the ones sitting in the front. What he happened to see shocked him – a Brahmin child sitting with a Muslim boy! It was unacceptable to him. He looked at them in disbelief before asking Little Kalam to stand up and tell his name.

'Abdul', said Little Kalam meekly, humiliated.

"Gather your things and move to the back row," the teacher said in a stern voice.

Little Kalam wanted to protest, but he could not. As he gathered his books and things, his eyes welled up. He wondered what happened, he was the star of his school.

As he stood up, he looked at his friend. He saw tears trickling down his cheeks. An attempt was being made to cut through the community; it could not go unreported, decided the two children.

□

Three Great Hearts Resolve a Problem

Problems are common, but what is important is the way they are tackled. A humiliated Little Kalam shared his woe with his father.

"This could not be acceptable if all communities have to live in harmony," Jainulabdeen murmured to himself. As he went to the square for his usual meeting with Fr. Bodal and Shastrigal, he noticed that Shastrigal was agitated. Ramanadhan, too, had reported the matter to his father. Jainulabdeen's had even more respect for Shastrigal. It was their harmonious spirit that had brought the three men together.

The three holy men were shocked and dismayed, and also, a bit agitated. This prejudice was against the grain of what they had worked for so far. They were even more desperate because it concerned a teacher, who was supposed to open up students' minds.

That same evening, the teacher was summoned to the square. The teacher was told in no ambiguous terms that the scourge of religious division would not be allowed to be instilled in the minds of the people in the town. Children, despite all the differences, could not be divided and segregated. That religion was meant to unite people, not divide them. That the cultural bond had to be inclusive, not exclusive. They warned the teacher politely but firmly of any communal agenda that could have a negative impact on the delicate minds.

The teacher apologized and said, "I acknowledge my divisive deed. I am sorry I had not thought of the consequences that could result following my action. I have seen the society around me structured like that, and I tried to introduce it here too, but I was wrong. I beg your pardon. It would not happen anymore."

The teacher left. All through the dialogue, he was dealt with dignity and respect. It was necessary to make him realize his mistake, but there was no intention to disrespect him. This was a lesson for everybody. If there was something that needed to be resolved, people should come together and talk firmly and openly and settle the matter amicably in the highest spirit. The Constitution of India was yet to come into being at that time, yet the three great hearts resolved the problem in the spirit enshrined in the Constitution.

□

Fancy for Science

Little Kalam was known for his aptitude for science. His favourite subjects included science and mathematics. He had been brought up in a spiritual atmosphere in which all three communities mingled with each other subtly, while still retaining their individuality. By the time he completed his eighth standard, he knew several things that were in the Koran. He also knew about many things that were part of the Geeta as well as the Bible. Together, they made him a product of this unique land of India.

He looked forward to attain a higher education in science, so he looked for avenues. Jallaluddin and Samsuddin helped him find more about the opportunities in different places, the nearest of which was Ramanathpuram, not so far away.

□

Mother the Homemaker

Little Kalam was one of the 10 siblings in the family, but Ashiamma, his mother loved him dearly and showered him with the deepest of her affection. She was frail, yet he found her to be the toughest woman. It was time that Little Kalam had to leave home for further study. He could not continue to be his mother's little boy. Food was rationed, yet his mother often gave away her own share so that he could have enough. He noticed this one day, and asked, "Why do you do this? You are weak and you have to do a lot of work in the house."

"You are my growing child," said Ashiamma taking his head in her lap and tenderly running her fingers through his hair, "You are a growing child, you have so much to do all through the day. This is what mothers look out for, don't worry about me."

Little Kalam was now a responsible and sensible adolescent. He could see how his mother worked relentlessly to run the household with so many children. Besides her own children, there were often relatives' children who came to stay with them. Feeding all of them was not an easy task, but she did it happily, never complaining.

□

Seagull Flies Across the Sun

Little Kalam wanted to go to a bigger school in a different town to study and realize his dreams. At the same time, he wanted to stay with his father and mother and siblings and friends. He was afraid of the kind of challenges and atmosphere he would have to face outside. This made him uncertain. His father read his mind and said, "Abdul, I know you have to leave home to grow. Does the seagull not fly across the sun, alone and without a nest? You must forego your longing for the land of your memories to move into the dwelling place of your greater desires. Our love will not bind you, nor will our needs hold you."

Little Kalam heard his father's prophesy earnestly and made up his mind. His father turned to Ashiamma and said, "Khalil Gibran said your children are not your children. They are the sons and daughters of life's longing for itself. They come through you, but not from you. You may give them your love but not your thoughts, for they have their own thoughts."

□

Lesson at the Railway Station

Little Kalam was at the railway station waiting for the train. Jallaluddin was going with him to get him enrolled in the Schwartz High School at Ramanathpuram. As they heard the whistle of the approaching train, Jainulabdeen tapped on Little Kalam's shoulder and said in a solemn voice, "This island may be housing your body but not your soul. Your soul dwells in the house of tomorrow, which none of us at Rameswaram can visit, not even in our dreams. May God bless you, my child!"

Little Kalam studied in his hometown up to the eighth standard. He now needed to explore the wider avenues outside. Jallaluddin recognized the fact that he could not be nursed in the small town anymore.

It was a lesson for a lifetime for Little Kalam. He had to chart the course of his destiny himself. He had to create his destiny through his work, and in this bid, he had to bring glory to his family, island, nation and world.

□

Sister Zohra

With so many children in the family, the children never knew what boredom was. They were a bunch of happy children. They would often quarrel, but would patch up soon to come up with some innovative game and they were all there to help each other.

Little Kalam found his sister, Zohra, the most affectionate after his mother. She was one of the older children in the house. She studied, but was expected to help her mother with household work. As the two toiled together for the family, they were more like friends—cooking and cleaning and looking after the young ones.

Unlike the other children in the family, Little Kalam was quieter and would often curl up with a paper or a book, rather than play or plan a prank with others. If he was not reading, he was dreaming. Zohra ensured that no one disturbed him.

In the times to come, she was the person who would help Little Kalam tide over difficult times.

□

Little Kalam Goes to Town

The town of Ramanathpuram was unlike his hometown, which was rustic in essence. The atmosphere at the new school seemed strange and unwelcoming, but he was here with a mission, that was to better the fortunes of his family and friends. So, he set down to focus and study.

This school was a stark contrast with Little Kalam's primary school at Rameswaram where a student was treated like an extended family member.

Instead, the new town was a thriving urban hub with little social coherence and harmony. He found it difficult, but he had a lesson in mind. To bloom, you need to either adapt yourself to the situation, or adapt the situation to yourself. He was not yet in a position to adapt the situation to himself. So, he decided to adapt himself.

□

Implications of a Gift

His father, Jainulabdeen was a holy man. He was man of noble qualities. When the Panchayat Board elections were held, he was elected as a member, and at the first council, he was elected the chairman of the Rameswaram Panchayat Board. He was not elected to this post because he belonged to a certain community or he spoke a particular language or he belonged to a particular economic class, but because he was a man of fine human qualities. In a few days, Little Kalam got a taste of his noble qualities, but the hard way.

During the winter vacation, Little Kalam visited his hometown. It was afternoon. He sat in the courtyard reading a book. There was a knock at the door. Little Kalam noticed that a stranger walked in with an impressive packet in his hands. He stood up and bowed in reverence.

"Where is your father?" the visitor asked.

"He has gone for namaz," said Little Kalam.

"I suppose I am getting late," said the visitor. "I cannot wait here. I am leaving this packet here, please give it to him."

"Please wait for a while," said Little Kalam softly. "I'll ask Mother about this."

Little Kalam went inside for his mother's consent, but she was praying. He returned to and told the visitor, "Better if you can wait. I don't know, but I think you can leave the packet here if you are in a hurry."

The visitor left the packet on the cot and walked away. Little Kalam went back to his book again. He looked up from his book only when his father came back and asked him about the packet.

"A visitor had come. He left this for you," said Little Abdul.

"Who was he?"

"I didn't ask his name," said Little Kalam realizing his slip.

Jainulabdeen was furious. He picked up the cane and beat him hard. It was only on few occasions that he had beaten him in his life. His mother rushed to save him.

Little Kalam wondered what provoked his father. When his father cooled down, he sat near his son touching his shoulder in affection and said, "Son, a gift puts a person under obligation. This man will return some day to ask for a favour, which he might not be eligible for. This will make things complicated."

Little Kalam realized the intricate implications of a gift. His father quoted from the *Hadith* and said, "When God appoints you to a high position, He takes care of you. If you seek anything beyond it, it is an illegal gain. A gift is given with a motive. So, it is like a poisonous snake. If you touched it, it would degrade your thinking."

Little Kalam later rose to a very high position in his life, but he followed this advice all his life.

□

Little Kalam Feels Homesick

Little Kalam was studying at the Schwartz in Ramanathapuram. It was for the first time that he had crossed the confines of the small town of Rameswaram. He wanted to study at a higher school in a different town, and at this juncture, it was Jallaluddin who made all the necessary arrangements. He travelled with him to Ramanathapuram and ensured that he settled down.

"This is a funny, strange place," said Little Kalam when Samsuddin was preparing to go back to Rameswaram.

"Yes, change is the law of nature, it is the law of life," said Jallaluddin like a philosopher. "If things remain constant and stationary, life will rot. You cannot allow water to stand stagnant. It has to flow to keep fresh. You have lived near the sea until now. You have seen that water keeps flowing. You are like seawater. You have to keep moving."

"Yes, I know," said Little Kalam seriously. "But I'll miss my family, my familiar surroundings, my mother and her cooking."

"You have your roots in your family, you must not forget your family members at any point in life," said Jallaluddin. "But you have to convince that you are away

from them for their good. You need to control your emotions in order to achieve a better education."

Whenever Little Kalam felt homesick, he recalled these words. He derived courage and motivation from them. He needed to come to terms with his life in a boarding school.

□

Reading Habit

Little Kalam was somewhat of an introvert boy. He interacted with others only as much he needed to. He found good company in books.

Soon, he came across a revolutionary nationalist, S.T.R. Manickam, who had a large library at his home, and was always willing to lend books to Little Kalam. The little boy was drawn to him out of innate curiosity, and soon found solace in the company of great books. It was in this library that he happened to read some fine books, including *The Law of Success* written by Napoleon Hill, a celebrated American writer. He was greatly motivated by what the book professed, especially when it said that the mind can achieve anything that it can conceive and believe. This mantra was to stay with Little Kalam all his life.

□

The Mentor and the Support

Little Kalam had a mentor in Jallaluddin, who encouraged and motivated him. He tried to answer all his queries. At home, he found the greatest support from his sister Zohra. While he studied at the Schwartz High School at Ramanathpuram, the two got married. They had their own household to manage, but the two were determined to ensure that Little Kalam gave wings to his aspirations.

Little Kalam was growing up to become an intelligent adolescent. Yet, he was called Little Kalam because of his inquisitive mind and endless questions. He wanted to become an engineer. So, he wanted to take admission at the Madras Institute of Technology (MIT) in Madras (now Chennai). The finances were, however, the biggest impediment. His father, who had to run a huge household, did not have a large enough income. It was still dependent on the ferry business, and the fee at the MIT was a whopping Rs. 600. Today, it may sound a paltry amount, but in those days, it was indeed a big amount.

It was at this juncture that his mentor and support came to his rescue.

Little Kalam was at home when Zohra visited. She

took him aside and asked, "What are your plans now? I want you to become a fine professional."

"I want to be an engineer, in fact, I want to be a fighter pilot," he said.

"Go for it," said Zohra.

"How can I?" said Little Kalam in an anxious voice, "How can I pay the fee? Where will the money come from?"

"We'll do everything we can," said the resolute sister. "I'll mortgage my jewellery."

"I can't let you do that," said Little Kalam thoughtfully. "We are passing through uncertain times, your gold is a safeguard for you. It is like an insurance policy on which you can rely during a crisis. You are no longer single. You are married and you have a family of your own to look after."

"You need not worry on that count. Trust in God and everything will be fine," assured Zohra patting his cheek.

She used her jewellery as security with a moneylender to borrow the required money. So confident she was of his capabilities. The brother too did not fail her.

Little Kalam proved with his hard work that her faith in him was not unfounded. He studied hard, earning a scholarship.

Zohra was a source of inspiration for Little Kalam. She always thought of her parents, brothers, sisters, husband and children first, and thought about herself the last. Her dreams and aspirations were fulfilled in the success of others. She was happy to see others happy. She had a lesson for Little Kalam. Serve others selflessly and God would ensure that everything goes well.

□

Little Kalam Goes Vegetarian

In late 1940s, Little Kalam was studying at MIT (Madras Institute of Technology). He had little money to spend on himself. Back at home, he was used to eating non-vegetarian food, but he knew that his father could not afford lavish expenses. He had barely managed to get admitted, thanks to her sister. He could not put any more pressure on the family. He was already studying hard with an eye on the scholarship, and needed better nutrition. With a modest budget, he decided to stick to vegetarian food.

"Let me try this vegetarian food," Little Kalam said to himself. It was cheaper and could help him save some vital money.

"It is weird," Little Kalam remarked when he first had a vegetarian meal in the mess. But, when he continued to eat it, he found it so tasty that he remained vegetarian all his life, and preferred simple food. We have several instances to quote from his life about his choice of simple vegetarian food. He was in Patna staying at the Inspection Bungalow. In the morning, the cook served him butter toasts.

Dr. Kalam asked him, "Don't you have anything edible? I don't want an English breakfast, I want something Indian—simple and relishing food." The cook boiled rice and pulses, which Dr. Kalam relished greatly. □

Little Kalam Writes an Essay

Little Kalam loved to read, but he realized that only reading could not help him organize his thoughts on a logical plain. His professor advised him to write extensively.

"What should I write?" Little Kalam was a little confused.

"Anything you like to write, it will help you shape your thoughts," said the professor.

Little Kalam started writing. In the beginning, he did not know what to write. So, he wrote about his daily routine, his class, and then he rose above these petty topics and started to write.

He did not preserve the pages he wrote, but he found that writing helped him. He was able to do his class work more easily than ever before. He now loved to note down his views and ideas and opinions.

Once in an essay competition, Little Kalam wanted to write on a topic which, he thought, could not have been chosen by anyone else. In his wild dreams, he wanted to be a fighter pilot. So, he chose a new topic, *'Let Us Build Our Own Aircraft'*.

At that time, India did not build its own aircraft and

was lagging behind industrially, scientifically and technologically. An essay on this topic gave a glimpse of his inner mind. Of course, he wrote this essay in Tamil. Surprisingly, he won a literary prize for it.

□

Little Kalam Misses Mother's Recipes

Little Kalam sometimes felt homesick. He wanted to be in the company of his family members, but at the same time, he also missed his mother's cooking. He was a great fan of his mother's *sambar*, which had the aromatic qualities of all the ingredients she used. He also missed *poli*, a south Indian sweet his mother used to make at home. She could make 12 different varieties of the sweet, each of them delicious and mouth-watering. In the beginning, Little Kalam availed himself of every opportunity to visit Rameswaram, but gradually, he stopped doing that because it impacted his studies. Also, he could not afford it.

At the same time, Little Kalam realized his family's hopes resided in his hard work. He could not undermine them. He was determined to put his desires to rest if he could realize his family's dreams.

□

Little Kalam Fails

Little Kalam was studying aeronautics at MIT to realize his dream of becoming an engineer. He worked hard. On one occasion, his design teacher, Professor Srinivasan, assigned students—each in group of four—a project of a low-level attack aircraft. Little Kalam's team was assigned the aerodynamic design. All the students worked hard, undertaking study and discussion in a bid to impress their professors. A few days later, the professor wanted to check on Little Kalam's progress. When he did, he said with displeasure, "This is just not good enough, boy."

Little Kalam was taken aback, but the professor continued sternly, "I expected much better from you. This is hopeless, I am disappointed."

Little Kalam had always been a star student. This assessment came like a shock, he was dumbfounded, ashamed and embarrassed.

"Re-do the design," the professor said and before turning away said, "You have three days to do it!"

"Yes, Sir," said Little Kalam. He was already going over in his mind how to get going in such limited time, when the professor turned back and dropped a bombshell, "Three days means three days, and should you fail, your scholarship will be stopped."

Little Kalam was devastated. The scholarship was the only way he could afford to study engineering. He was unable to think for some time, and then he came to terms with the first shock of his life. He recalled the words of Jallaluddin, who had once said, "When you feel desperate, the best way is to start the work and sink yourself in it."

This is just what Little Kalam did. He thought over his entire project, and with it, new ideas started to float in his mind. In no time, he was working like a man with a mission. In two days, he completed his basic design, and from the third day, he was busy finalizing it. He was working at his desk, when he sensed somebody's presence in the room. He glanced from the corner of his eyes. There was a shadow to his right. He turned and found his professor standing before him.

Little Kalam wondered what the professor was doing there. Three days was yet to get over. The professor looked critically at his work for some time, and then hugged him affectionately saying, "You are on the right track."

"Thank you, Sir," said Little Kalam greatly relieved.

"I set you an impossible deadline, but you have impressed me with excellent work. I pushed you to your limits so that you could recognize your potential," said the professor.

There was one, rather two lessons in this incident. A teacher can push his students to stretch and excel. But, only he should know when to push and when not to.

When later in life, Little Kalam was engaged in teaching, he avidly followed this practice. The second lesson was even more important – there is nothing like an impossible deadline. If you are committed to your work and ambition, no goal is out of your reach. Little Kalam, as a rocket scientist later in life, proved this when he built satellites and launched vehicles within assigned rcsources and time.

□

विवाह
प्रस्ताव

Little Kalam
Decides to Remain Single

Today there is a legal bar on child marriage. Boys and girls are not supposed to marry before they attain a certain age. However, when Dr. Kalam was a child, when he was Little Kalam, child marriages were in vogue, and in keeping with the tradition, a proposal came from Sivaganga for a marriage alliance. When he came to know of this, he resigned himself to loneliness to speak to himself. He asked himself, "What do I really want in life? Will marriage help me attain my goals or will it prove to be a barrier?"

Little Kalam contemplated this topic for a while and then he decided that his goal, his ambition was near his heart, he could not sacrifice it.

"How to convey it?" Little Kalam thought deeply.

"There can be two ways," Little Kalam said to himself, "One is to come up with some excuse so that any decision can be deferred for now. Another is to reject the idea outright."

He weighed the pros and cons and chose the latter. He decided that he would not marry, and stuck to this decision throughout his life.

□

Little Kalam was Spiritual

Since his early days, Little Kalam lived in a spiritual atmosphere. His father, Jainulabdeen was a thoroughly religious man. He would never miss his prayers, nor would he allow his kids to miss theirs. For any query, he would refer to the holy texts, and find the apt answer. For him, spirituality was not in religion alone. It was to be found in every sphere of one's life.

Little Kalam, who was born and brought up in the temple town, grew up amidst spirituality. During the times when he slipped his way into the ferry boat, he came to know of astounding mythological tales from Hinduism. The ideas from Hinduism and Islam blended to offer a harmonious mix, and then there was an element of Christianity too.

Fr. Bodal often sat with his father and discussed matters of the world, including spirituality. For them, religion was a uniting force. It could not separate or tear apart.

Yet another friend of his father was Pakshi Lakshamana Shastrigal, who often related interesting tales about Gods and Goddesses.

All these influences stayed with Little Kalam when he left his hometown. Whenever he got an opportunity, he wanted to find out about vivid manifestations of spirituality from religious and spiritual men. He found that all these were diverse ways to attain the same Truth, the same Conscience, the same Learning. He wanted everybody to realize this.

□

Little Kalam Learns Lesson of a Lifetime

Little Kalam was about to leave town for further education, when his father, Jainulabdeen gathered all his children and sat together. He said, "You may look for clean jobs, but it is dirt, the earth that ensures our long life and traditions."

Little Kalam, like many of his siblings, did not understand what his father was trying to say. Jainulabdeen noticed their confused faces and explained, "Those who tend to live a life of expensive habits can prosper for a generation or two. Those who are industrious and frugal, like merchants, can prosper for three generations or four; those who till the ground with simple habits can think of living for five or six generations; but the longest to live are the people who remain true and respectful to their families, elders, ancestors and friends."

Little Kalam had a lesson to learn from this statement – Never be cruel and never be rude to anyone.

□

Surprise Honour

It was Little Kalam's last day at MIT. He had passed with flying colours, and all his batch-mates and professors had lined up for a group photograph as part of the farewell ceremony. The professors sat in the front row while the students lined up behind in three rows. The photographer arranged everything and before he hid himself behind the black cloth of his camera, he said, "Attention, please smile."

Just then, Professor Sponder stood up and said, "Wait a little, please."

Everybody was surprised at this interruption. Prof. Sponder was a senior member and very professional in his approach. He was known for shaping his students keenly. He was known to be someone with a humane touch and fine qualities of a teacher. He apologized and said sorry when he realized everybody was looking at him.

He turned around and looked at the rows, trying to spot Little Kalam in the last row. He said, "Kalam, come and sit with me. You are my best student and I am confident you will bring glory to your teachers. You deserve it. May God bless you."

As Little Kalam staggered from the last to the front

row and the professor created a place for him to sit with him, everybody clapped.

As everybody stood up to disperse after the photograph, Prof. Sponder said, "Kalam, your voyage to the wide world begins now. Undertake it so everybody will be proud of you."

Little Kalam only nodded with a polite smile. He was sure that his teachers' blessings would serve him in good stead.

□

Little Kalam Fails Again

Little Kalam was no more 'little' now, he had passed his engineering course, but we will continue to call him Little Kalam because of the fact that he had a delicate, child-like, curious mind. It was 1957.

The problem in India is that one cannot be sure if one can surely make a career in his chosen field, so one has to often choose from a range of alternatives. Little Kalam had to face this dilemma. He wanted to be a fighter pilot, but he knew he needed a back-up plan.

So, he also applied as an engineer with the government. He appeared for the interview in Delhi, and then went ahead to Dehradun to appear for the test to be a pilot with the Indian Air Force. He cleared the initial tests and did his best for the remaining group tests and GTO tasks. In the merit list, he ranked ninth, while there were only eight vacancies. He was shattered. He looked for solace in spirituality. So he went to Rishikesh, where Swami Sivananda guided him, "Forget this failure, it was essential to lead you to your true path."

Little Kalam had a lesson to learn from this failure. It is destiny that shapes your life, but you have to work towards it. The holy man's words rang in his ears. The

Geeta tells us to work, for it is in our right to act, but the fruit of our actions are not in our hands.

And these words came true. On his way back, he found that he had been selected as an engineer with the government. With this, he set on a path that would make him a popular scientist globally. One who made rockets and satellites and rose to be the President of India —the People's President. He rose to be a personality who continues to be adored even after his death.

□

Little Kalam Owes Success to Teachers

Once during his later life, Dr. Kalam was asked who he owed his success to. He said, "I owe my success to my teachers, who directed me at various turns of my life."

Here we shall refer to a few instances.

The Caring Teacher

Rev. Fr. Sequiera taught English, but Little Kalam found it difficult to cope with the English medium instruction. "How can I do well?" he asked his teacher.

"It is simple," said the teacher convincingly. "Read novels and biographies." Not satisfied with this advice, the teacher also brought some books which could help his student.

Besides this advice, he also conducted additional classes in the evening. Little Kalam and some other students who were weak in English were able to grasp the language well in a month and a half.

Little Kalam Writes a Letter

Rev. Fr. Sequiera was on his evening round in the hostel, when he found Little Kalam sad and morose.

"What is the matter, Abdul?" he asked.

"Nothing, Sir," Little Kalam tried to smile, but failed.

"I know what ails you," said the teacher. He took out an inland letter from his pocket and gave it to him. "Write to home; I'll come and collect it half-an-hour later."

Pill for Headache

On another occasion, Little Kalam's roommate had a headache.

"What happened?" Little Kalam enquired.

"I have a terrible headache," said the friend.

"Okay, I'll bring you some medicine from the clinic," said Little Kalam.

He was about to go out when Prof. Sequiera dropped in. He asked in his cheerful voice, "Is everything fine?"

"Sir, he has a headache. So, I am going to the clinic," said Little Kalam.

"Don't worry about that. Here is an aspirin tablet, take

it and you will be all right soon," said the teacher to the ailing friend.

Scoring Good Marks

One question troubles every student, that is, how to get a good score. Little Kalam, too, wanted to know the secret. So, he asked his teacher, Prof. Chinnadurai.

The teacher said, "Long or short hours of study time does not make much impact. What makes the impact is how you study and what you read. If you thought you could score high marks by reading only notes or readymade notes from the market, you could not be right. You must read reference books and textbooks, and read as widely as you can during the initial period, and when the examination time is near, make notes from these books. Notes should serve you to remind points, and nothing more."

Little Kalam followed this advice earnestly.

Sanitation Inspection Rounds

Little Kalam loved to walk during his free time in the evenings. Often he walked around the city roads with his friend. He termed it as the sanitation inspection rounds. When his friend asked why he called it so, Little Kalam quipped, "We go around the city to see if all streets are cleaned well or not." The two friends then laughed their hearts out.

Recognizing Heroes

Little Kalam, in course of his study, found that many Indians were very successful in several fields, but they

did not get any credit. This fact perturbed him. He referred to Tipu Sultan whose Army used rockets even before the British knew about them. But no one knows who invented these rockets which wrought havoc on the enemy.

However, the British had a meticulous record of what

all William Congrave did to rocketry. He saw Tipu Sultan's Army use rockets and made use of the same technology against the French. The credit should have gone to the Indians. Instead, the foreigners hogged it.

Little Kalam thought that Indians did not perfect records and that was why India's history was not judiciously documented.

□

One from Grown-up Abdul

In this book, we have narrated several stories from his life—from his childhood until youth. Now, we shall pick one story from the days when he was a grown-up and the project director. This will tell you the way he dealt with his juniors.

There were about 70 scientists working on a project of national importance under the supervision of Dr. Kalam. The work was hectic and tedious, and could take months, but all of them were motivated to do their best.

Sometimes, they were frustrated owing to the pressure, but Dr. Kalam's inspirational leadership helped them to stay on the right course. They not only worked hard, but also had to work late into the evenings daily as they had to complete the project within a given time frame. But, there were occasions when they had to give into justified demands of their families.

In this case, a little child wanted to go to an exhibition in town. He impressed upon his father, a scientist working with Dr. Kalam on this project, to leave office early and take him to the exhibition. The scientist mustered courage and sought permission to leave early that day. Dr. Kalam consented with the well-known perennial sleek smile that always graced his lips.

But could the scientist go? No...he was so busy and engaged in his work that he forgot that he had to leave early. Finally, when he looked up to check the time, he was stunned to see it was way past the scheduled time. He knew he was in trouble. He looked for his Boss, but he was not there. He had taken permission to go early, but he was already late. So, he hurriedly wrapped up and left. He knew he would have to deal with an unpleasant situation at home, and he was trying to prepare himself for it.

Feeling guilty, he stepped into the drawing room where his wife was sitting. He meekly sat down and waited for his wife to admonish him but he was unnerved when she calmly asked, "Would you like to have coffee or shall I straightaway serve dinner if you are hungry?"

This made the poor scientist even more nervous. He said softly, "If you would like to have coffee, I too would have it. But what about the exhibition?"

There was surprise in store for him. She said, "Don't you know? Your manager came and said that you were busy, and he took the child to the exhibition."

Apparently, at five o'clock, Dr. Kalam went to the scientist's cabin to remind him of his appointment with his child, but when he peeked into the cabin, he found him he was totally absorbed in his work. It was evident that he would miss the deadline.

So, Dr. Kalam went to his house and took the child to the exhibition.

From this and many more similar incidents, one learns the kind of man Dr. Kalam—Little Kalam in this book—was.

□

References

Books

The Very Best of A.P.J. Abdul Kalam – The Righteous Life, Rupa Publications India, 2014.

Forge Your Future, A.P.J. Abdul Kalam, Rajpal & Sons, 2014.

India 2020: A Vision for the New Millennium, A.P.J. Abdul Kalam and Y.S. Rajan, Penguin Books India, 1998.

A.P.J. Abdul Kalam: Scientist and Humanist, Atulindra Nath Chaturvedi, Rupa Publications India, 2002.

Songs of Life, A.P.J. Abdul Kalam, Ocean Books, 2015.

Ignited Minds, A.P.J. Abdul Kalam, Penguin Books India, 2002.

The Scientific Indian, A.P.J. Abdul Kalam and Y.S. Rajan, Penguin, Viking, 2010.

Wisdom of Kalam, Prashant Gupta, Ocean Books, 2012.

You Are Born To Blossom: Take My Journey Beyond…, A.P.J. Abdul Kalam and Arun K. Tiwari, Ocean Paperbacks, 2015.

You Are Unique, A.P.J. Abdul Kalam, Punya Publishing, 2012.

Turning Points: A Journey Through Challenges, A.P.J. Abdul Kalam, HarperCollins Publishers India, 2012.

Spirit of India, A.P.J. Abdul Kalam, Rajpal& Sons, 2010.

A Manifesto for Change, A.P.J. Abdul Kalam and V. Ponraj, HarperCollins Publishers India, 2014.

My Journey: Transforming Dreams into Actions, Rupa Publications India, 2013.

Governance for Growth in India, A.P.J. Abdul Kalam, Rupa Publications India, 2014.

The Family and the Nation, Acharya Mahapragya and A.P.J. Abdul Kalam, HarperCollins Publishers India, 2008.

Wings of Fire: An Autobiography of A.P.J. Abdul Kalam, Universities Press, 1999.

Reignited: Scientific Pathways to a Brighter Future, A.P.J. Abdul Kalam and Srijan Pal Singh, Penguin Books India, 2015.

Inspiring Thoughts (Inspiring Thoughts Quotation Series), Rajpal & Sons, 2007.

Advantage India: From Challenge to Opportunity, A.P.J. Abdul Kalam and Srijan Pal Singh Harper Collins India, 2015.

Transcendence My Spiritual Experiences with Pramukh Swamiji, Harper Collins India, 2015.

Beyond 2020: A Vision for Tomorrow's India, Viking, 2014.

My India: Notes for the Future, Penguin India, 2015.

You are Unique: Scale New Heights by Thoughts and Actions, Punya Publishing Pvt. Ltd., 2012.

Meri Jeevan Yatra, Prabhat Prakashan, 2014.

Thoughts for Change: We Can Do it, Pentagon Press, 2012.

Mission India: A Vision for Indian Youth, Puffin Books, 2005.

Guiding Souls, Ocean Books Pvt. Ltd., 2005.

The Luminous Sparks: A Biography in Verse and Colours, Punya Publishing Pvt. Ltd., 2004.

The Family and the Nation, HarperCollins, 2014.

Envisioning An Empowered Nation: Technology for Societal Transformation, Tata McGraw-Hill, 2003.

Vijayi Bhav, PrabhatPrakashan, 2011.

The Scientific Indian: A Twenty-First Century Guide To The World Around Us, Penguin India, 2010.

Sukhi Parivar Samriddha Rashtra, Prabhat Prakashan, 2011.

Bharat 2020 aur Uske Baad, Prabhat Prakashan, 2015.

Governance for Growth in India, Rupa Publications India, 2014.

Mere Sapnon Ka Bharat, PrabhatPrakashan, 2013.

My Life: An Illustrated Autobiography, Rupa Publications India, 2015.

A Manifesto for Change: A Sequel to India, HarperCollins, 2014.

Mission India, Penguin Books India, 2015.

Family And The Nation The, Harper Collins India, 2008.

Jagrat Bharat, Shreshtha Bharat, Prabhat Prakashan, 2013.

Websites

1. www.abdulkalam.nic.in
2. www.brainyquote.com
3. www.successstory.com
4. www.firstpost.com
5. www.dailyo.in
6. www.youthconnect.in
7. www.indiatvnews.com
8. www.india.com
9. www.quora.com
10. www.lifehacker.co.in